Things I Wish My

Mother

Taught Me

15 Strategies to Uncover Your Happiness

SUZANNE RIVARD

BALBOA
PRESS

A DIVISION OF HAY HOUSE

Balboa Press books may be ordered through booksellers or by contacting:

Balboa Press
A Division of Hay House
1663 Liberty Drive
Bloomington, IN 47403
www.balboapress.com
1 (877) 407-4847

Cover and Interior Illustrations provided by Danielle Caners.

Printed in the United States of America.

ISBN: 978-1-4525-8318-1 (sc)
ISBN: 978-1-4525-8327-3 (e)

Library of Congress Control Number: 2013917398

Balboa Press rev. date: 01/14/2014

Dedication

This book is dedicated to my mother, who provided me with a loving and safe environment growing up, full of opportunities and potential. I would not be writing these words today if it weren't for her. I admire the strength and courage she doesn't even realize she has at overcoming life's challenges. I have had the privilege of being witness to the personal growth she has undergone over the last few years.

I love you, Mom!

Happiness is a conscious choice,
not an automatic response.

—Mildred Barthel

Happiness is a conscious choice,
not an automatic response.

—Mildred Barthel

Contents

Preface

Over the years I have had moments where I struggled to believe in myself and kept myself small. It has been a lifelong journey to build the belief and trust in myself, a journey that will continue until I leave this physical world.

I chose the title *Things I Wish My Mother Taught Me* because these are life lessons that I had to learn experientially. The title is not a reflection on my mother's skills as a parent. My mother did an amazing job raising three children. I simply wish my mother had been given this handbook when she was growing up, and she could have passed it on to me.

Having this handbook would have eased my internal struggle, avoided many tears and painful experiences. It would have provided me with a blueprint to create more happiness in my life, fast-tracking me to success and happiness.

I have worked through the different strategies at various times in my life. Reflecting on my experiences four themes emerged. I grouped the strategies into these themes to provide you with your blueprint for success and happiness.

Before you begin this book, I want to share with you the poem that has been the most inspirational to me. It's about the power of your thoughts and what you believe in yourself. It's a philosophy I live my life by. Several years back I recited the poem during a job interview. I got the job! I didn't find out until years later how some in the interview panel had also been moved the poem. I'll bet you'll find it as inspirational and moving as I do.

Suzanne

Thinking
Walter D. Wintle

If you think you are beaten, you are;
If you think you dare not, you don't;
If you like to win, but you think you can't,
It is almost a cinch you won't.

If you think you'll lose, you're lost,
For out of the world we find
Success begins with a fellow's will,
It's all in the state of mind.

If you think you are outclassed, you are;
You've got to think high to rise.
You've got to be sure of yourself before
You can ever win a prize.

Life's battles don't always go
To the stronger or faster man;
But soon or late the man who wins
Is the man WHO THINKS HE CAN!

Acknowledgments

I would like to thank all the people that have crossed my path, many of whom were my teachers. Without them, the lessons and experiences they brought me, I would not be the person I am today. I am very blessed!

Special thanks to my mother, Estelle, and father, Norm, for providing me with a life of opportunities. To my brother, Phil, who is always there for me when I need him. To my sister, Michelle, for sharing this life journey with me and expanding my horizons. To my niece, Danielle, who is the most grounded young lady I have ever known, for her belief in me and for her amazing artistic capabilities, which she shares with us through the illustrations found throughout this book. She is an inspiration to many!

Thanks to my friend Jamie Fehr, who has been a support for me over the last year. He has encouraged me to grow, to follow my dream, and to write this book. To my friend William Porter, for assisting me with the editing.

And finally, thanks to Donna Kozik for providing me with the structure, support, and initial editing in writing this book.

Who Is Suzanne Rivard?

Suzanne Rivard grew up in the Canadian prairies, where she lives today with her dog, Emma.

She has a bachelor's degree in computer science and worked in the information technology industry for over twenty years. She has always had a passion for helping people. Even when she was hired for her first job after completing her university studies, she was asked why she was choosing to work with computers rather than people.

She has traveled extensively throughout the world and has had the privilege of interacting with people of diverse cultures. Some of the many places she has explored are Australia, New Zealand, Europe, Egypt, Thailand, Japan, and Central and South America. She spent one year living in the Canadian Arctic. Through her travels she developed openness, acceptance, and kindness toward all people.

After many life experiences, she chose to leave the corporate world and embrace working with people exclusively, supporting them to heal, grow, and achieve their dreams. She has embarked on a career as a personal coach.

Twelve years ago Suzanne suffered an injury that resulted in surgery around her tailbone. The surgery was successful, but many muscles, nerves, and tissues were permanently damaged. As a result she suffered severe back issues and sciatica, and has had difficulty walking. According to doctors, the only solution to alleviate the pain would be cortisone injections into her spine for the rest of her life. That solution was not an option she wanted to pursue; thus, she began her search for alternative healing solutions.

Her pursuit became a passion and a curiosity to learn about various healing modalities. She has studied and practiced Chinese massage, huna, and various forms of energy healing, including Reiki. As part of her own personal growth, she studied meditation and t'ai chi. She spent a month in an ashram in India studying yoga.

In 2005 an incident occurred which shook Suzanne to the core. She experienced deep suppressed anger arise within her until she was in a rage. She had no idea where all the anger was coming from, as she is not an angry person. Unsure and scared, she reached out to a therapist to help her heal emotionally.

Since then she has sought out assistance from various therapists and coaches. So impressed with how they transformed her and her life, she explored various modalities at even deeper levels. She became a certified hypnotherapist, master neuro-linguistic programming (NLP) practitioner, master time line practitioner, life coach, health coach and law of attraction coach.

She believes that seeking help along your life's journey is not a sign of weakness but one of strength. You don't need to go it alone. You're choosing to be courageous to heal the past, grow, and become a better version of yourself.

In 2011 her passion transformed into a dream career in which she teaches others and shares her knowledge. Suzanne's mission is to teach people to connect with their highest potential.

Her philosophy of wellness is about finding fulfillment and balance in all aspects of one's life. She refers to herself as an integrative wellness coach, empowering her clients to lead a more fulfilled, balanced, and meaningful life, starting from where they are in the present moment. She provides a safe and supportive environment for them to achieve their goals and dreams, partnering with them to end their internal struggle and create the life they want.

To find out more about Suzanne and see what she's up to, visit http://www.SuzanneRivard.com

Introduction

Your thoughts are powerful! They influence how you feel about yourself and the world around you. They direct the actions you take and whom you choose to interact with. When you own your thoughts, you own your life.

Things I Wish My Mother Taught Me: 15 Strategies to Uncover Your Happiness explores personal strategies that focus on different aspects of you and your life. The strategies are grouped into four themes. The themes represent a balanced approach to one's life and one's happiness.

The first theme, *Master Yourself*, is about your thoughts and perceptions, what you think about yourself, other people, and the world. Your thoughts influence your emotions, your choices, your actions, and how you perceive yourself in the world. Learn to master your thoughts, increase self-love and self-belief, and let go of past hurts that are keeping you stuck. *Create inner peace and happiness.*

The second theme, *Live with Integrity*, is about discovering your emotions, taking responsibility for them and yourself, consciously choosing to focus your energy on what drives you and is important to you. Learn to honor yourself and your emotions, be honest with yourself and others, and take responsibility for yourself. *Promote harmony within yourself and your world.*

The third theme, *Feel Your Body*, is about the choices you make to support your physical body. You cannot survive without a body. The better the choices you make to take care of your body, the more you can partake in life and do the activities that bring you joy. *Energize your body and increase vitality.*

The fourth theme, *Nurture Your Relationships*, is about the relationship with yourself and the people you choose to share your life with—not feeling alone in the world. What you think about your relationships and what you receive from them has a huge impact on your soul, spiritual connection, and sense of belonging. *Develop heartfelt connections.*

The last section, *Uncover Your Happiness* (which isn't one of the themes), provides you with steps to determine how to start, narrow your focus, gain clarity, and identify actions to successfully adopt the strategies into your life. *Be the creative force of your life.*

Each strategy has an exercise for you to do. Doing the exercise enables you to adopt the strategy in your life, discovering new awareness about yourself, your actions, and your thoughts. With your new self-awareness, you'll make better choices and create the life you want and deserve.

This is a book that you'll refer to many times as you adopt the various strategies.

THEME I

Master Yourself

STRATEGY #1

Start with Gratitude

Gratitude is the best attitude.
—Anonymous

Everything starts with gratitude!
Too often we're caught up in our everyday lives. We're busy and never take time to slow down, to appreciate the beauty and all we have. Most of us in the western part of the world are extremely fortunate. We don't have to worry about food, clothing, shelter, or safety. Our fundamental needs are met. This is not true in other parts of the world.

Here we're trying to keep up with everyone else, acquiring material wealth for status, buying the latest gadget or upgrading our homes—all to make us feel better about ourselves. We feel the need to be the best, often at the expense of others. It's all about being number one and survival of the fittest. Having the lifestyle you desire is wonderful, but don't get lost in it or become defined by it.

Do you take the time to appreciate the people and things you're grateful for in your life?

You could be the most negative person in the world and think that nothing will ever change. That's not true. If you start being grateful for the people and things in your life, you'll begin to look at your life differently. Instead of seeing the negative in people or things, you'll start noticing the positive, the beauty. Your life will feel abundant. This is why you hear people talking about the importance of gratitude.

When you're great at noticing positive aspects in people and things, some may call you a Pollyanna. Don't let that deter you. Thank them for the compliment. Wouldn't you rather view your life as a place full of abundance and beauty than a place of negativity and despair?

I have had the privilege to travel to many places in the world. When I was in Indonesia, I was invited to a local Hindu wedding. It was in a remote village. Before the wedding my friend and I visited his family's home up in the mountains. The scenery was amazing, but that's not what stuck with me. Compared to western standards, the family has very little. Some would even say they're underprivileged and have a horrible life. Yet they were some of the happiest people I have met. They were grateful for the people and things in their lives and not focused on what they didn't have. They radiated happiness.

If you want to live a life of happiness, begin by noticing and appreciating the abundance and beauty that are already in your life; *be in a place of gratitude.*

Exercise

A great way to appreciate what you have is to keep a gratitude journal. You'll find many resources on what a gratitude journal should be or contain. I have pulled together what I believe to be the best of the best. Adjust the content to meet your needs and desires. For instance, a client of mine preferred to keep a happy journal rather than a gratitude journal.

1. Get yourself a journal and write down things you're grateful for.

2. For the next thirty days, every day write down five (more if you're inspired) people or things you're grateful for.
   - It takes twenty-one days to form a habit. By completing this exercise for thirty days, you're giving yourself the opportunity to shift toward a life of abundance and happiness.
3. Gratitude is not about you; it's about people and things in your life.
4. It's important to write down the gratitude.
   - This gets you completely focused on one thought, the gratitude. It gives the gratitude power, a higher energetic vibration. The higher the vibration, the more you'll attract people and things to be grateful for.
5. The gratitude should be as specific as possible.
   - The more specific you get, the more energy you put behind the grateful feelings you're having. Try to be specific to the point where if you read it in the future, you can remember the actual moment.
6. After you have written the gratitude, read it out loud to yourself and feel the gratitude.
   - Feeling gratitude brings more of it into your life.
7. Some people struggle with this activity. If this is you, start small, but start. Write one or two gratitudes per day, in more general wording, and build up from there.
8. Challenge yourself to not repeat your gratitudes. Make each and every one of them unique.

When you're feeling ungrateful or down, pick up your gratitude journal and read to yourself out loud what you have written. It will remind you of special moments and people in your life. It will shift you into feelings of gratitude—a higher energetic vibration.

Esther and Jerry Hicks introduced the teachings of Abraham and the Law of Attraction in the book *Ask and It Is Given*. These teachings are the foundation of the movie *The Secret*. Based on Abraham's teachings, it takes seventeen seconds to start shifting your vibration toward gratitude, and sixty-eight seconds for the vibration to be strong enough to start attracting more people and things to be grateful for in your life. Take your time, read, and deeply feel the energetic vibration of gratitude.

Tip: A gratitude journal is a great tool to use all the time, not just for thirty days.

STRATEGY #2

Change Your Perception of the World

If you don't like something, change it; if you can't change it, change the way you think about it.

—Mary Engelbreit

*L*et's face it—there's lots of negativity in the world. You only have to watch the news or read the newspaper to see stories of murders, wars, and tragedies. Lots of people start off their day reading the newspaper and setting their tone for the day. If they read some negative stories, they carry those with them for the entire day. They talk about them at coffee break, over lunch, with friends and family. Some people choose to watch the news at night before they go to bed. What do you think they dream of?

What do you think reading and watching the news does to your perception of the world? It's a scary place, right? Well, it doesn't have to be. *You can choose what you allow into your world and what you focus on.*

You might be saying, "I need to keep informed of what's going on in the world," and "There are positive, uplifting stories." You're right. In fact, keeping informed is a good thing, but you don't need to inundate yourself.

The focus on negativity has an impact on how people operate in the world. Deepak Chopra says that on average we have fifty thousand thoughts per day, with most of those being negative in nature. If most of those thoughts are focused around negativity, life appears bleak.

A few months ago I was out for lunch with my mother. She started telling me about a tragic accident that happened on the highway, in which a young lady lost her life. A young man was driving the vehicle that collided with the young lady's. There was question as to whether or not alcohol was involved. Bless my mom's heart—she is a deeply compassionate and caring person. When she was telling me all of this, her entire body was feeling it. Her energy was low. She felt the pain of the loss of the young lady and the judgment against the young man. Her body language clearly showed the emotions she was feeling. I asked her, "How does focusing on this make your life better?" She was kind of jarred and replied, "It doesn't." So I said, "Why focus on it, then?" She chose to let it go. Her entire physiology and energy shifted back to enjoying the lunch and conversation we were having.

Don't get me wrong. I'm not saying that having empathy for people is bad. All too often we're empathetic with attachment. We're reacting to the distress of another human being. We feel their pain, and we also take on that pain emotionally and energetically. At times this can be appropriate. However, it can also be very disempowering to an individual. If you're a deeply caring person and you take on everyone else's pain, you're suffering more then you need to be.

What you focus on impacts you, your mood, and your energy. The choice is yours.

Exercise

To notice the impacts of negativity on you from the world around you, start by eliminating the news sources from your awareness.

1. For seven days, don't read any newspapers or watch the news.
2. After seven days, notice how you feel.
   - Do you feel you're missing out?
   - Do you feel better, worse or the same?
   - Has not keeping up with the news had any impact?

After seven days, if you want to remain informed, limit the amount of time you read the newspaper or watch the news. You may want to completely eliminate those sources and selectively choose the news stories you want to read on the internet. My preference is to hear about the news through conversations with people. You choose what is best for you.

Get Rid of the Negative Self-Talk

> The body, like everything else in life, is a mirror of our inner thoughts and beliefs. Every cell within your body responds to every single thought you think and every word you speak.
>
> —Louise Hay

*M*ost people have a very negative image of the world and, worse, a negative image of themselves. They've never fully learned to love or embrace themselves; they don't live to their fullest potential. *Learning to love yourself for who you are can change your life.*

We're hardest on ourselves. We limit and sabotage ourselves with labels like "I'm stupid!" and "You idiot!" or saying phrases like, "Why did I have to do that?" and "It's never going to get better, so what's the point?" Would you treat a good friend that way? Remember: fifty thousand thoughts per day. Just imagine how all those limiting thoughts and beliefs are impacting you.

Religion can be supportive but can also be detrimental to an individual. My own experience of being raised within the dogma of a religion negatively impacted my self-esteem and self-worth. I was taught, for instance, that I was born a sinner and was not worthy. These limiting beliefs about myself created many challenges in my life. I no longer accept them as true.

Believing I was a sinner caused me to second-guess myself. I couldn't make any mistakes. Yet I always seemed to and had to repent for them. I never believed that I was a truly good person. I now know this is not true. Every day I strive to be the best version of myself, and that demonstrates my goodness. *Everything is an opportunity to learn and grow from*; mistakes don't make me a sinner.

The belief that I was not worthy held me back from achieving my potential and fully embracing who I am. I held myself back because I didn't deserve. I kept myself small. Nowadays I stretch myself all the time. I'm deserving of the best life I can create.

Each and every one of us is amazing! We all have unique gifts to offer the world. We all matter and have value. It's said that for every person born there were a thousand souls that wanted to take the body, competing for the job. The fact that you are here, that you got the job, means that you have value. Yes, *you have value*!

We all are meant to be here. You're here for a reason. What you offer to the world is up to you. You may not have figured out what your gifts are yet. That's okay. Life is a journey. It's all about the journey and not the destination. You'll figure it out. In the meantime, stop being so hard on yourself. *You're doing the best you can from where you are and what you've been taught.*

Have you ever thought, "What's the point to my existence? I don't matter. Life would be better without me. Nobody would miss me. I don't make a difference in other people's lives." Well, I have, and it's not a great space to be in. When I'm in this space, I focus on something in the future that I'm looking forward to or some happy memories. I keep doing this until I shift out of it.

One of my favorite movies that reminds me of the role we all play in the world and how we make a difference in other people's lives is *It's a Wonderful Life,* starring James Stewart and Donna Reed. In the movie, George Bailey, played by Stewart, experiences some great challenges in his life. He gets to the point where he feels like the only choice is to end his life. An angel comes down from heaven and gives him the gift of seeing the world as if he had never been born. All of the people whom he cherishes are all living out different realities. He realizes the difference he has made in all of their lives and asks to have his life back, woes and all. It's a great movie; watch it if you get the chance. It's on every Christmas.

Listen to the language you use with yourself. Do you often notice the words *should* and *need*? These are expectations you're putting on yourself, and when you don't follow through, you feel bad. Many people have too many "should's" and "need to's." They're never meeting expectations. How do you think this impacts them? They constantly feel like a failure.

Lots of negative self-talk is about disappointing others. We think that we should be this way or that way. We should be doing this or that. When we don't live up to those expectations, we get down on ourselves. We're trying to live up to other people's expectations of us, not our own. Are you living your life according to your expectations or someone else's? *Start living by your expectations.*

Everyone seems to be worried more about what other people think of them than about what they think of themselves. That often defines their behaviors, thoughts, and actions. Out of fear of judgment, they don't truly express who they are at the core. Learning to love yourself and embracing all that you are is foundational in leading a happier life.

I have heard said, "What others think about you is none of your business." *It's their perception of you and not who you truly are.* When you learn to honor yourself first and be respectful of others at the same time, the fear of judgment will disappear. Remember, if you don't want to be judged, then don't judge others. Everyone is doing the best they can from where they are in life.

When I was eight years old, my grade three teacher held a math quiz. All the students had to stand at the front of the class while she asked us math questions. If you got the answer wrong, you sat down. One by one, students took their seats until I was the only one left standing. She kept asking me question after question. I was up there for a long time. You'd think that was an awesome experience, but that's not what I held inside me. After the quiz, all the other students made fun of me and called me keener, goody-goody, and names of that nature. The experience left me scarred and terrified of standing in front of a crowd. Now I overcome the fear and do it anyway. Have you ever had a similar experience?

Through our experiences we take on limiting thoughts and beliefs about ourselves.

Exercise

To discover the negative language you use with yourself, your labels, and the limitations you put on yourself, start paying attention.

1. For seven days notice the language you're using with yourself. Pay close attention.
   - Writing down your negative and limiting language will help you identify patterns. Don't judge yourself harshly; it's simply where you are right now. You're changing that!
2. Ask yourself the following questions.
   - Are many of my words negative?
   - Am I labeling myself?
   - Am I putting any limitations on myself?
   - Do I have negative beliefs about myself?

3. Challenge any limiting thought or belief you have about yourself by asking the following questions.
   - Is it true? Is it absolutely true?
   - What does holding onto this serve me?
   - Who would I be without this?
   - What would my life be like without this?
4. Compile a list of all the negative words you're using.
5. Cross out the negative words, and replace them with empowering ones of your choice. For example, instead of saying "should," replace it with "choose."

Carry your empowering words with you as a visual reminder. When you catch yourself using a negative word, repeat what you said with a more empowering word. Over time, you'll express empowering words naturally without effort or thought.

Tip: A great tool to bring you acute awareness of your negative thoughts is to wear a rubber band on your wrist. Every time you say negative or limiting words, snap the rubber band. It works!

STRATEGY #4

Acknowledge Yourself

Believing in yourself is a choice.
—Suzanne Rivard

What are you good at? What are your strengths?

We all have strengths. Yours are unique and different from others. Too often people claim that they aren't good at anything or don't do anything right, continually dismissing who and how amazing they truly are. *You have strengths whether you acknowledge them or not.*

We compare ourselves to others and put ourselves down because we aren't as good as they are. We don't focus on what makes us great. We feel like we're never enough. *You are enough!*

Everything you need to be great is already inside you. Maybe you express your greatness, and maybe you don't. Start celebrating who you are now.

What are your accomplishments, your successes, and your wins?

People often have a hard time listing any accomplishments. They say they have never achieved anything of value or get anything done. That is not true. We all achieve things and succeed at something we set out to do, even if it's a small thing like getting a cup of coffee. We go throughout our day not realizing all that we're achieving. We're so busy and forget all that we've done. All the small things add up to a much bigger whole. We get caught up in a picture of what a successful life should look like, what we think our family or society expects of us, what we need to do before we pass from this lifetime so that our life has meaning.

Acknowledging my achievements is something that I have struggled with on and off. I always felt that I needed to get married and have children. I'm not sure if my family or society implied those beliefs. Regardless, I have done neither.

When I went to my high school reunion, I felt like a failure because I hadn't achieved either. I completely dismissed that I successfully completed a computer science degree, had a great job, had some wonderful relationships, and got to travel the world. At the time all those things didn't seem to matter. I strive to accept who I am and where I am at and continue to do so on a daily basis. I choose to embrace all that I have done and all the possibilities I have for the future. There are gifts in everything if we choose to see them. Marriage and children may or not be part of my life in the future, and that's okay.

What about yourself are you most proud of? What do you admire about yourself?

Most of us have a hard time receiving compliments from others, myself included. We dismiss them and don't believe them to be true. People don't give compliments just to give compliments. They're taking the time to say something nice about you. We think that we're being modest by not accepting the compliment. We're actually putting ourselves down and dismissing the other person's offering.

If you think about it, compliments are a reflection of what others see and think about you. They're praising you or something you've done. *Appreciating you for being you!*

If you aren't used to accepting compliments, they may feel fake or even make you uncomfortable. You may have been raised to not be open to them, because accepting them means you're full of yourself, or maybe growing up you simply never received compliments. You have never learned how to fully embrace them. It doesn't matter, because from this point forward you can choose to receive them.

The next time you receive a compliment, fully receive it and say thanks. Don't worry if you catch yourself dismissing it; we all do at times. Simply regroup yourself and say, "Thank you." Opening yourself up to receiving takes time and practice. Just keep at it. Receiving compliments is a great thing.

Giving compliments is also very rewarding. When you give a heartfelt compliment, words of encouragement or admiration, you can make someone's day. It can make such a huge difference. You don't know how their day is going or what's happening in their life. For someone who feels unloved, who has no one there for them or may be struggling today, your words and belief in them could change their life.

Several years ago I was working through a self-help book. One of the exercises was to compile a list of things that you're grateful for and admire about someone. I chose to write them about my sister. When I was done, I sent her my list. She phoned to thank me and said that it was exactly what she needed at that time.

Don't forget to give yourself compliments. *Praise yourself for who you are!* This is vitally important, because if you don't compliment and believe in yourself, it will be challenging to embrace praise and support from others.

Acknowledgments can take on many forms: strengths, accomplishments, self-praises, compliments, and recognition from others. Focus on acknowledging and praising yourself for all the things that you're doing right, and celebrate your greatness. You'll view yourself differently and *transform at your core.*

Exercise

To uncover your greatness, keep an acknowledgment journal.

1. Get yourself a journal, and for the next thirty days write down acknowledgments:
   - successes and wins, even the small ones
   - things that you get done
   - things you do well
   - things you are proud of
   - actions taken toward your goals
   - compliments from others
   - things people praise about you
   - self-praises and compliments
2. Be open to and receive compliments from others.
3. Give yourself kudos, like "Way to go!" and "Great job!" Write those down with some context of what they refer to. This may be challenging at first but will get easier with time.
4. If you find this a struggle, start with the small stuff, like "Today I smiled and at someone, and they smiled back." Just keep writing in your journal every day.

When you're in a space where you feel like you never accomplish anything and aren't good at anything, or are just down on yourself, pull out your acknowledgment journal and read it out loud to yourself. It will shift what you think others think of you and how you see yourself. You'll be more open to embrace all of the great aspects of yourself. Absorb all of the things that you have accomplished and your praises, all that you do, and how far you have come toward achieving your goals. Give yourself a pat on the back rather than being hard on yourself.

Note: Notice the patterns of things you do well. These are some of your strengths.

STRATEGY #5

Forgiveness Is Key

> Without forgiveness life is governed by . . . an endless
> cycle of resentment and retaliation.
>
> —Roberto Assagoli

*O*ne of the biggest things you can do for yourself is forgive yourself! We hold onto so much sorrow, and it's not healthy. We all have regrets and disappointments that happened, sometimes many, many years ago. We hold the emotional pain as if it just happened. The emotional pain is stored as negative energy in the body and causes blockages; blocked negative energy leads to stress and poor health.

It's important to remember that we're all doing the best we can from where we are in life. The experience of life is different for each and every one of us. The way we are and operate in life is a direct reflection of our beliefs, values, thoughts, memories, and experiences, our perception of what happened. Our entire past has formed us into who we are today, and if we let it, it will define our future too.

When you do something to hurt someone, the best thing you can do is to tell him or her that you're sorry and didn't intend to hurt them. When you genuinely apologize to someone and they accept it, both of you can let go of it and move past it. Conflicts are a natural dynamic in a relationship. Apologizing will strengthen and deepen your relationship.

Forgiving others is also vitally important. We hold onto past hurts. He or she did this to me, or this or that was wrong. Holding on is having a bigger impact on your life than theirs. All of that negative energy is stored in your body. These hurts are hot buttons just waiting to be pressed. Something completely unrelated could set them off. When that happens you're right back in the negative energy of the past. I'm sure that you have experienced that for yourself at times. We all have.

Do you think that the other person is living his or her life thinking about how he or she hurt you? Probably not. By not forgiving, you're holding onto that every day. Forgiving is not condoning what happened as acceptable or right. *Forgiving is for you.* You don't need to keep holding onto that negative energy. You can move forward in your life without being triggered and reliving the past.

Some say, "I will never forgive them. Their behavior is simply unforgivable." It's not about forgiving their behavior. Rather, it's about releasing that negative energy within you so that it no longer impacts your life. You cannot change the past. You can learn, grow, and move forward from it. *You don't need to keep living in the past.* It's a choice.

Forgiveness of others is something that I always strive for. It just makes life so much better. I feel good about all the people in my life and those that have passed on in my journey. They have been my greatest teachers. I hold no resentments.

They say that others are a direct reflection of you, your mirror. They're in your life to teach you about you. It's up to you whether you accept the lessons.

Everyone is doing the best they can. When someone hurts you, you don't know what's going on with him or her. They may be having a bad day. Maybe they just lost their job or someone has died. They may be treating you like they treat themselves. You just don't know. Everybody's actions are meeting some kind of a need. It may not even be about you at all. I like to give everyone the benefit of the doubt.

If you're disappointed or hurt, honor your feelings and look at the situation from a different perspective. Ask yourself, "What can I learn from this experience?" and "What gems are in here for me?" There are no mistakes, no failures. Everything is an opportunity to get feedback, to learn and grow from. Experiencing what you don't want gives you clarity about what you *do* want. It's what you make of the challenges presented to you that matters, not what happened in the past. Rather than staying stuck in the past, *use your experience to build a better future.*

Some people feel like the life they had envisioned was taken from them. They were powerless to stop it. They hold someone responsible for that. They're feeling forced to live a life they didn't want and are stuck in the thoughts of what their lives were supposed to be like. They aren't able to let it go, and they live in the past. They're hurting, angry, and constantly suffering.

This often happens to people who get divorced. After a divorce it's important to grieve and heal; it's a loss. Too often people remain bitter for life; they don't forgive. They don't give themselves the gift of dreaming of what could be. They're stuck in the past instead of looking at the infinite possibilities of the future. They are not embracing who they're free to be and the amazing life they can have.

You're probably thinking that there are just some mean people out there who want to hurt you. You're right. When I encounter those people, I tell myself that it's about them and where they are in life; it's not about me. I choose not to hold onto what they have said or done. I don't let it bring me down. If it's someone important in my life, I do my best to openly communicate with him or her so that we can get past it. If it's someone that simply is negative and is not significant in my life, I choose to distance myself from him or her and let it go.

During a hypnotherapy session I experienced a process that enabled me to release negative energy stored in my body. You go back along your timeline, your life experiences, to the moment when you first suppressed the negative emotion, learn what was important to learn at the time, and then release the emotion. That moment is no longer a trigger for you, and the negative energy is no longer stored in your physical body. You have gotten the lesson, and you have let it go.

One of my sessions was particularly powerful. Early in the week I had stopped to pick up some coffee at a local coffee house. A car pulled up beside mine, and the driver hit my car door with his. I mentioned that he should be more careful. He was flippant and dismissed me. From inside me this anger arose. I was so angry that I was physically shaking and just wanted to hit him. This was not like me. I had no idea where all this anger was coming from. I was in a rage. It scared me. I got help. I chose to work with a hypnotherapist, who used the process with my timeline. In the session, I was able to release the anger. The emotional charge of the anger took several hours to work its way out of my body, and by the next day I was a whole new person. I never learned the source of the anger, and that doesn't matter. What matters is that I was able to release it.

Forgiving yourself and others can be challenging to many. *A good place to start is with forgiving yourself,* and then move on to forgiving others.

Exercise

A safe and powerful way to forgive yourself and others is by expressing your feelings through the written word: a forgiveness letter.

1. Write yourself a letter.
2. Address the letter to yourself in the third person.
3. Write down all of the things that you have done to hurt yourself and how they hurt you, followed by what your life will be like when you release that hurt. Write the things that you have suppressed and need to express.
4. Finish off the letter by writing, "I am now ready to release this hurt. I forgive you!"
5. Don't show anyone the letter. It's for your eyes only!
6. Go somewhere private and read the letter out loud to yourself. Absorb the words. Feel the emotions. Don't suppress them. If you need to cry, then cry. If you need to yell, then yell. Do whatever you need to do to allow the emotions to be released and flow. It's time to let them go.
7. When you're done, destroy the letter by ripping it up in little pieces. Some people like burning it.

Now that you have forgiven yourself, write a letter to someone else whom you're ready to forgive. Repeat the process described above. If you have many people to forgive, write a letter to each and every one of them.

If writing a forgiveness letter is not enough for you, and you're not able to let go of the hurt, you may want to consider seeking out additional support from a therapist, counselor, or some other professional who can assist you.

Summary

THEME I
Master Yourself
Create Inner Peace and Happiness

Strategy #1: Start with Gratitude
Strategy #2: Change Your Perception of the World
Strategy #3: Get Rid of the Negative Self-Talk
Strategy #4: Acknowledge Yourself
Strategy #5: Forgiveness Is Key

Master Yourself is about how you view and feel about yourself and the world. People who focus on negativity live a difficult and challenging life. People who focus on positivity live a happier life.

Changing your perspective and how you think will transform your life. It's not about just telling yourself, "Today I'm going to be positive," and replacing the bad with the good. It's about taking action: changing your thoughts to more positive ones, being kinder to yourself, acknowledging yourself, being open to receiving, and letting go of past hurts. You crowd out the bad with the good, changing your thought patterns at your core.

This is not something that will be accomplished overnight. It has taken you many years to get to where you are today. It's about *starting your healing journey here, now, today!* The more you're able change your perspective; the more your life will improve. Stop beating yourself up. Be gentle with yourself.

THEME II

Live with Integrity

STRATEGY #6

Discover Your Emotions

Your emotions are the slaves to your thoughts, and
you're the slave to your emotions.
— Elizabeth Gilbert, *Eat, Pray, Love*

ots of people go through life in reactive mode. They
allow life to direct them instead of choosing the life they
want. They feel like they have no control over anything;
life just happens. They don't realize that they're going through life
on an emotional roller coaster.

Emotions are natural. We all have them. One emotion is not
more or less important than another. Emotions gauge where we are.

Rather than suppressing an emotion, it's better to let it play
out in a healthy way, riding the wave, so to speak. When someone
is angry and they're told it's wrong to feel that way, often they
suppress the anger. They aren't permitted to express it and are left
feeling like they're wrong for feeling that way. Take someone who
is depressed, for instance; they rise out of the depression and now
feel angry. Those around them tell them that the anger is wrong.
Instead of expressing the anger and getting past it, they suppress it
and fall back into the depression.

Growing up, we're taught what's right or not right to express, and how to express or not express emotions. Those around us model this. Men are taught not to cry, that crying is a sign of weakness. Crying is natural for all of us. It's about releasing sadness and grieving in order to heal, letting go of your attachment to what you have lost. What's so wrong about that?

In some families individuals aren't allowed or encouraged to express their emotions in healthy ways, while other families express their emotions in unhealthy ways. We all have different experiences of how to process emotions based on our upbringing, experiences, and beliefs.

Growing up, I didn't talk about my emotions, nor was it encouraged. As an adult I struggled with expressing and processing my emotions in a healthy way. I didn't even know why I was experiencing an emotion or what is was about. I was reactive to everything. I didn't express how I felt, and everything was always bottled up inside me, ready to explode. Expressing and processing emotions is an aspect of myself that I have worked on a lot—still do, to this day.

Through self-observation I discovered how often my emotions change. That knowledge helps me not be attached to what I'm experiencing. I allow the emotion to flow and do not suppress it. I honor what I'm feeling and don't judge myself for it. I do what I need to do to allow that processing, whether that be taking some time to myself, journaling, or communicating with someone when I'm not as emotionally charged.

Knowing and understanding your emotions empowers you to respond rather than react. Allowing you to be in control.

Exercise

To discover the fluctuations in your emotions and identify your primary emotions, you have to pay attention to them.

1. For seven days, write down what emotion you're feeling every half hour.
    *   Yes, that's right: every half hour. It may seem like too daunting a task. Yet I urge you to do it. It will be life changing.
    *   Optionally, you can choose a fifteen-, forty-five-, or sixty-minute interval. However, thirty minutes is optimal.
2. There are many different emotions. Below you'll find some examples.
    *   If you have trouble putting a label to your emotions, do some research on the internet or in books. There are many sources with more comprehensive lists of emotions that you can reference.

You'll discover what your most frequent and primary emotions are and how often your emotions change. Knowing where you are emotionally is important to be able to move forward, take action, and heal if you need to. Enabling you to identify and process your emotions in a healthy way without suppressing them. You may also choose to seek further assistance if you are struggling emotionally.

Tip: This tracking technique can be used for many applications, such as what you are spending your time on, to discover your time wasters.

Emotions

HAPPY	UNHAPPY	UNEASY	ANGRY
awesome	ashamed	anxious	annoyed
comfortable	depressed	apathetic	cross
confident	despairing	awkward	disgusted
content	devastated	bored	enraged
excited	down	confused	frustrated
grateful	humiliated	discontented	furious
hopeful	hurt	embarrassed	irritated
overjoyed	lonely	flustered	jealous
peaceful	lost	frazzled	livid
pleased	miserable	insecure	overburdened
proud	rejected	nervous	pissed off
relaxed	sad	stupid	scared
relieved	self-conscious	uncomfortable	trapped
surprised	upset	weak	used

Take Responsibility for Yourself

When you change the way you look at things, the things
you're looking at change.

—Wayne Dyer

What are your hot buttons? What is it that people do or
say that causes you to react?

We react without being aware of why. We're
responding to the moment without conscious awareness. Having
better awareness of your emotions, as we explored in the previous
strategy, and your hot buttons, enables you to have better control
of how you respond to other people. How you respond is a choice,
your choice. *Awareness is the first step in being able to choose how to
respond.*

It takes two people to create the dynamics in a relationship. It's
a two-way street. Each person feeds off of the other's energy and
responds accordingly. Ever notice how a disagreement can quickly
escalate into an argument where both people are super-charged?
Neither one is open to hearing how his or her actions contributed
to the situation.

The next time you catch yourself blaming the world or others,
take a step back to reflect. Hindsight can be very helpful. When

you're in the moment, it's hard for you to identify your contribution. What was your role in the outcome? Perhaps there's an alternative solution that would work better. What can and are you willing to let go of? What and who are you able to forgive—perhaps yourself? What can you do differently next time?

Have you ever run into people that are never at fault? They blame the world, circumstances, and other people for everything that happens in their lives. They seem to have an excuse for everything and never take any responsibility for themselves. There is always some reason they behaved a certain way—and it's not them. They're a victim of the world and their circumstances, a martyr. It isn't a very empowering place to be.

This is different from a trauma victim. If you have experienced a deep trauma in your life and feel victimized, you want to give yourself the opportunity to heal. There are many great therapists, counselors, other professionals, and organizations that provide excellent support to those with deep suffering. You don't need to suffer alone. They can provide you with a safe, supportive environment to process the trauma and heal. Find one that you feel safe and connect with, that aligns with your values and beliefs.

If you're feeling that in your life everything happens to you and you have no control, if you view yourself as a victim, you want to choose to shift your perspective to one of empowerment. Doing so is about changing how you view yourself, your situation, and your life. The strategies described in the *Master Yourself* theme and this theme will definitely shift your perspective of the world and how you operate in it. When you change how you operate in the world, your relationships and your world change around you. Things will get easier and be less confrontational. It's about *changing yourself, not others.*

One of my favorite personal development movies is *You Can Heal Your Life*, by Louise Hay. She is an inspiration to both young and old. This movie is based on the concepts that changing your thoughts and taking responsibility for yourself can change your life. It's a movie that changes lives. My sister and I were so impressed with this movie that we got it for our parents.

You're responsible for your life. Make it everything you want it to be.

Exercise

To take responsibility for yourself and your actions, ask yourself some powerful questions. Take the time to reflect deeply on your answers. You don't need to share your answers with anyone. To bring deep awareness, be completely honest with yourself—no censoring.

1. What are you a victim of?
2. What do you get out of being a victim?
3. Who will be the "winner" or "loser" if you get your way?
4. What are your hot buttons? What triggers an emotional response from you?
5. What happens if you continue your present behavior?
6. What's the problem?
7. How important is this to you in the bigger picture?
8. What do you want the rest of your life to be about?
9. What is missing for you right now?
10. What would you like to change?
11. What do you want people to remember about you?

Having the answers to these questions will bring you awareness. With that awareness you have more power to choose how you respond to others and situations in your life.

Live by Your Values

When you are content to be simply yourself and don't compare or compete, everybody will respect you.

—Lao Tzu

D o you know what your values are? Do you live by them? *People who live by their values every day have more fulfilling lives.* They're meeting their deepest desires and putting their energy into the things that are the most important to them. They don't feel like they have wasted their lives, time, or energy.

Not living by your values can lead to frustration, destructive behavior, and even self-sabotage. Determining what your values are and living by them can have a huge impact on your life.

Not all values are equal. They're in a hierarchy according to the priority, or importance, you assign to them. You have some overall life values. You can also have different sets of values for different aspects of your life, such as work, family, spirituality, social life, and health.

Some people experiencing life challenges have incongruence with their values. They may not even be aware of the source of these challenges. Others have conflicting values between different aspects of their lives. Identifying their life values and those in the different aspects would be extremely insightful—reassessing what's important to them. Changing their values and priorities to meet their current needs would have a life-changing impact, bringing balance and harmony.

Values aren't set in stone. As you go through life, they may change. Their importance may increase or decrease, depending on where you are in life.

When you know your values, you can live a life of congruence.

Exercise

To determine what your life values are, ask yourself the following questions, and list values that are important to you. Below you'll find a list of common life values that can help you if you're unable to determine what your values are.

Identify Your Values

1. What is most important to you? Keep asking yourself, "What else?" Often our most significant values are deep inside of us and aren't the first ones that we think of. Keep repeating "What else?" until you have expressed them all.
   - If you respond with a goal, ask yourself, "And what do I want through having that?" or "What do I value in that?"
2. If you were well advanced in years, what kind of words would you most appreciate family and friends saying about you and your life?

Identify Your Top Ten Values

3. Out of all the values you identified, pick your top ten.
4. Determine the priority of your top ten by taking one value as the starting point.

5. Compare the next value against that one. Ask yourself which one is more important, and assign the priorities.

6. Take your next value. Compare it against your highest priority value, and ask yourself which is more important. If it's more important, then it goes above the one you just compared it to. If it's less important, compare it against the one you previously had as the lower priority, and place it accordingly. Now you have your priority for three of your values.

7. Take the next value and compare it to the values you have already prioritized, and place it in the correct priority. Do this until you have prioritized all ten values.

8. When you have your list of values, ask yourself, "Do any of the challenges in my life seem logical now that I look at this list?" and "Is there a better way of prioritizing my values so that they would fit my current needs?"

   • If you answered yes to the second question, then determine the best priority for you in this moment.

Your Top Five Values

9. Write down your top five values, and display them somewhere where you see them daily. Focusing on more than five spreads your energy too thin. Some people choose to focus on only the top three.

10. Align your actions with your top five values. Every day strive to perform actions that support each of the values. If you miss a value one day, address it the following day.

Tip: If you're experiencing incongruence in a particular aspect of your life, or are simply curious, repeat this process to identify your values for that particular aspect.

Common Life Values

accomplishment	freedom	originality
affection	friendship	passion
agility	fulfillment	peace
awareness	fun	perseverance
balance	generosity	power
beauty	growth	privacy
commitment	harmony	productivity
compassion	health	protection
connecting	helpfulness	punctuality
contribution	independence	realism
courage	integrity	reliability
creativity	intimacy	respect
decisiveness	intuition	security
discipline	leadership	service
encouragement	longevity	simplicity
fitness	love	sympathy
endurance	mastery	toughness
enthusiasm	mindfulness	trust
faith	modesty	uniqueness
family	openness	wisdom
flow	organization	youthfulness

STRATEGY #9

Find Your Purpose

If you can't figure out your purpose, figure out your passion. For your passion will lead you right into your purpose.

—T. D. Jakes

What drives you? Why do you get up every day?

Often when people are struggling to find purpose in their lives, they aren't following their passions. They're at a loss and find it difficult to get up every day. Even when someone feels quite grounded with their thoughts and how they feel about themselves, if they don't have purpose, their lives can still be challenging.

Purpose can be defined regarding the task at hand or the overall theme in your life. The purpose I'm referring to here is your life purpose.

Your purpose can change throughout the different aspects and phases of your life: childhood, marriage, parenting, work, and retirement. Not everyone has the same life experiences. *Your purpose is unique to you.* It's something that you must determine. They say that elderly people with pets tend to live longer. They have a sense of purpose: to love and care for their pet.

Maybe you don't know your purpose and are still discovering it. Following your passions is a great way to give your life some purpose, a sense of meaning. These are things that bring you joy, that drive you. They bring excitement into your life. Also, focusing on your vision of your future can be a tremendous help, giving you direction to move toward every day.

Over the years I have done lots of personal development. Yet at times, I have felt like something was missing. I questioned myself frequently. *Why am I here? What do I want to do with my life? How can I make a difference?* I have thought about these things a great deal over the last year. I have redefined my purpose. I want to reach out and touch as many people as I can, facilitating their healing and growth, so they create more happiness within themselves and their lives.

Discovering and knowing your purpose brings peace and joy into your life. It gives you a sense of meaning and a reason for living, a cause bigger then yourself, something to look forward to every day.

Exercise

Reflect deeply on these questions; they will bring you insights into your purpose.

1. For whom are you living?
2. Whom do you serve?
3. How do you touch people?
4. Why do you exist?
5. What are you passionate about?
6. What brings you joy?
7. How did you make a difference in the world today?
8. What's your future vision for your life? For yourself?
9. What's your legacy?

Suzanne Rivard

Summary

THEME II
Live With Integrity
Promote Harmony Within Yourself and Your World

Strategy #6: Discover Your Emotions
Strategy #7: Take Responsibility for Yourself
Strategy #8: Live by Your Values
Strategy #9: Find Your Purpose

By developing awareness of your emotions and hot buttons, you put yourself in a much better position to be able to handle all situations without reacting to them. Taking responsibility for yourself and your actions is more empowering then being reactive and a victim to the people and the world around you.

Living your life by your values and on purpose will bring you a much more fulfilling and rewarding life.

When you honor yourself and your feelings, and choose your actions and where you put your energy, you become the creative force in your life. *You're engaged in your life and not just living it.*

38

THEME III

Feel Your Body

STRATEGY #10

Slow Down

Health is a state of complete harmony of the body, mind
and spirit. When one is free from physical disabilities
and mental distractions, the gates of the soul open.
—B.K.S. Iyengar

*T*oday our lives are fast-paced, compared to the lives of
our grandparents and those before them. Everything and
everyone is moving so fast, trying to squeeze everything
into every possible moment. We lead busy lives, and for those with
children, they're even busier. *We forget to slow down.* It's no wonder
that most people are extremely stressed and not able to relax.

It's important to take some time for yourself. Some use the
television to tune out from their everyday reality; that works to a
certain extent. The problem is that most watch too much television
rather than taking some down time for personal care, which would
be more rejuvenating.

What have you done for yourself lately? Did you take a bath,
maybe go for a walk, or connect with a friend? There are so many
things that you can do for personal self-care. It's all a matter of
preference. Not everything will appeal or rejuvenate everyone the
same way.

What rejuvenates you? *Do something for yourself today.* Check out the list of personal self-care ideas at the end of this strategy. Brainstorm some new ones of your own to add to the list.

Pets are great for slowing down. They're always in the present moment. Playing with your pet or taking them for a walk can be a great way to slow down and be in the moment.

You hear about meditation everywhere. It's a great technique for slowing down. The simple mention of the word sends many people running. They heard and believe that meditation is for chanting Buddhist monks who can clear their mind of all thoughts— or for new agers or spiritual people—but not for them. Or they try a particular form of meditation and find that their brain is in overdrive and can't focus. Coming to the conclusion that they're doing it wrong or aren't cut out for it, they then stop meditating all together. There are many forms of meditation, and everyone can do it.

Meditating is simply self-regulating your focus of attention. It's nothing to be scared of. Meditation can be as simple as listening to music you enjoy, walking in nature, gardening, or attending a t'ai chi or yoga class. It's narrowing your focus and letting go of your everyday thoughts. Some meditations are guided visualizations, and others are self-directed.

If you haven't tried meditation, do so. Meditation has so many benefits. It gets you out of your everyday thoughts and stresses. Your body physically releases tension. You'll shift from operating out of your sympathetic nervous system—fight or flight—to operating from your parasympathetic nervous system, responding from a place of balance and wholeness. Pick a form that you're drawn to, or maybe experiment with a few. Discover which ones work best for you. Which ones do you enjoy the most? When you enjoy something you're more likely to do it.

Some general guidelines for meditation:

- When you're meditating and realize that you're off on a thought tangent, simply notice it and come back to your focus. Do not beat yourself up over it. It's natural. Some call this the monkey brain.
- Your focus level can vary from day to day, depending on what's happening in your life. This is normal. Over time and with consistency, it will get easier. You'll be able to be more present in the moment.
- In sitting meditation, it's better to start with five minutes a day, rather than doing a meditation once a week for thirty minutes. Consistency is a key. Start with smaller increments of time, and build up to longer periods: ten, twenty, or sixty minutes.
- The best time for meditation is first thing in the morning or just before bed. This is when your brain is most receptive and in an alpha state. If those times don't work for you, do it when you can. Doing is better than not doing.

Focusing exclusively on your breathing is also meditation. One the best stress-release activities you can do is to breathe consciously. There's an entire branch of the eastern Ashtanga yoga called Pranayama. It's all about breathing and using the breath in various techniques.

If you're new to meditation and want to explore guided meditations in more depth, a great book is *Creative Visualization* by Shakti Gawain. How she explains the process and the guided visualizations she gets you to explore are easy even for the beginner. She has an anniversary version that includes a CD with guided meditations from the book.

Slowing down and taking time to rejuvenate will not only release stress but also get you more grounded within yourself. *Giving you more balance.*

Exercise

Do this simple breathing technique to develop your comfort level with meditation and release stress at the same time.

1. Sit in a comfortable position.
    - Some prefer to lie down; if you tend to fall asleep when you lie down, then sit up.
2. Make your spine as straight as possible to allow the energy to flow.
3. Breathe in deeply through your nose, and exhale slowly through your mouth.
4. Inhaling for three to four seconds, completely fill your lungs.
5. Exhale for twice as long.
6. Keep focusing on your breathing.
7. If your thoughts drift off, simply bring your focus back to your breathing.

Even three breaths like this can release stress. Aim for five minutes to start, and build from there. Notice how much more relaxed you become.

Personal Self-Care Ideas

be a tourist in your own town

buy yourself flowers

connect with family and friends

cook a nice meal

cut technology use or even go "unplugged"

dance

eat slower

enjoy nature

exercise

garden

have a bath

listen to music

make time for yourself

meditate

read a book

say no to requests that don't feel right

sit for a moment with your eyes closed when you're feeling stressed

start a journal

take a class

take a nap

take a walk

volunteer and assist someone else

watch or go to a movie

Note: There are additional benefits to narrowing your focus and being in the moment, not worrying about the daily stresses. You become connected with yourself and can accomplish amazing feats.

A great movie about being in the present moment, the now, is *Peaceful Warrior,* starring Scott Mechlowicz and Nick Nolte. A college gymnast's world is shaken to its core when he shatters his leg in a motorcycle accident. He learns how to embrace where he is, and what he can do, the power of being in the present moment and not worrying about anything else.

After watching this movie, I applied its concepts to myself during a recreational game of volleyball. When I was serving, I focused on just being in that moment, nothing else. I served twenty-one points in a row. It was absolutely amazing and powerful!

STRATEGY #11

Move Your Body

Take care of your body. It's the only place you have to live.
—Jim Rohn

Not only do we lead busy lives, but also many of us are sedentary. We travel from place to place via a vehicle and never walk much. When we get home we sit down in front of the television for the entire evening. The more we are sedentary, the less motivated we are to get up and get moving. The less we move, the more sedentary we become. It's a vicious cycle, and it takes action to break the pattern.

Being active does not mean you have to run a marathon. It means getting your body moving to keep it agile and away from stiffness. Movement keeps your muscles, blood vessels, heart, and all your other organs active. Strength training puts on bone mass, which increases bone density.

Take a walk. Go to the gym. Maybe there is some new exercise class that you have wanted to check out. Don't wait! Do it as soon as you can. It doesn't have to cost you any money. Walking, yard work, and gardening are all great activities to get you moving. Get involved in recreational sports like volleyball or baseball. They're excellent activities to get you mobile and you get to socialize at the same time.

When I was in Nepal, I took a guided hike up a mountain through some local villages. This was quite the physical challenge for a girl from the Canadian prairies, which has a flat terrain. As I was huffing and puffing my way up the mountain, an elderly women walked by at a fast pace. She was carrying a heavy load in a bag strapped around her head. It was inspirational to see. You're never too old be fit and active. You just need to do it.

Yoga is a great form of exercise, as it's meditative and improves your flexibility, balance, and strength. Not all yoga classes are equal; find an instructor and a class that you enjoy.

If physical activity is new to you, start slow and build up to doing an activity every day. Ideally you want to combine some forms of exercise that are a bit more rigorous and get your heart pumping, with some that are less demanding on the body. If you have concerns, consult with your doctor before starting.

Moving your body is vital to its longevity!

Exercise

If you're struggling with what to do, start by identifying things that you enjoy doing that are active.

1. Some possible activities are listed below. Brainstorm some on your own to add to the list, or make your own list.
2. Pick one activity you enjoy that gets you moving, and do it this week.
3. If you find it challenging to motivate yourself, find a friend to do it with.

The more you get active, the better you'll feel.

Activities

aerobics	skating
badminton	skiing
baseball	skipping rope
carrying stuff (from children to groceries)	soccer
	squash
cycling	swimming
dancing	t'ai chi
golf	volleyball
gym	walking
hiking	weight training
house cleaning	yard work
jogging	yoga
running	

Fuel Your Body

If you don't take care of yourself, the undertaker will
overtake that responsibility for you.

—Carrie Latet

We're so busy that at times we forget to eat. *Fueling our
bodies with food is an essential part of their functioning.*
Many people entirely skip breakfast—the most
important meal of the day. I'm one who in the past never ate breakfast,
but breakfast starts your body off with energy to face the day.

What we eat is also important. Fast foods and packaged foods
tend to be nutritionally poor. Junk food causes our blood sugar
levels to spike and drop. We experience mood swings and low
energy. Ever wonder why you're so tired at work after eating lunch?
At three o'clock you need a pick-me-up, so you eat a chocolate bar.
You get some energy temporarily, only to feel yourself crash again
not that long after.

Foods impact different people in different ways. One food may
energize one person and achieve the opposite for another. The best
thing is to experiment to find out what foods are best for your body.
This is why some of the diets you hear about work well for some and
do absolutely nothing or are harmful for others.

Following a specific diet for medical reasons is a great thing. Following one for a fad or to lose weight quickly is not healthy. A diet may reduce or eliminate essential food groups and/or nutrients. A person typically will return to their old eating habits and lifestyle after a certain period of time. If the diet was restrictive and they lost a lot of weight, their body probably thought they were starving. Their body wants to protect them and now stores excess fat to prepare for the next time they're starving, building up reserves for self-preservation. This is why some gain more weight than they lost after following one of these diets.

The best approach to changing your diet is to move toward whole foods and preparing the meals yourself. Experiment and see what you like and don't like. Discover what foods fuel you and what foods deplete you. Adopt the foods that are working for you into your lifestyle. Your healthy changes will be sustained, as you have changed your entire approach to eating for life. *You'll have a healthy dietary lifestyle in the long term and aren't just following a diet.*

Following an 80/20 rule makes a new dietary lifestyle achievable. For 80 percent of the time you eat healthy, and the other 20 percent, if you choose, you allow yourself to have the cake or treat you desire, without feeling guilty. You don't feel like you are depriving yourself. *It's all about balance.*

Another important aspect is hydration. Did you know that 80 percent of most people's aches and pains could be reduced or eliminated simply by drinking enough water? Most people are extremely dehydrated. Drink more water and see how you feel.

Sleep is also important. When we don't get enough sleep, we aren't operating at peak. We become sluggish and have brain fog. Our bodies use sleep to rejuvenate themselves. Many people are so busy that they don't allow themselves enough time in their schedule to get adequate sleep. If this is you, allow yourself at least one full night sleep per week where you don't wake up with the alarm. Your body will love you for it.

To fuel your body and improve your health, follow these simple guidelines.

- Drink more water.
- Eat more whole foods.
- Practice cooking.
- Increase whole grains.
- Increase sweet vegetables.
- Increase green leafy vegetables.
- Use good fats.
- Experiment with protein. Not all protein sources are equal or fuel your body the same way. Some prefer to stay away from certain sources for ethical reasons.
- Eat fewer processed foods.
- Get enough sleep.

Exercise

A great way to start your day is with a nutritious breakfast. How do your start your day? To figure out what foods fuel you best in the morning, do this experiment.

1. For one week, eat a different breakfast every day.
2. Alternate between different foods, such as fruit, cereal, porridge, and eggs.
3. Notice which breakfasts give you longer-lasting energy and keep you fueled. Which ones are leaving you hungry for more food or low in energy in a shorter time?

Incorporate the foods that give you more energy and keep you fueled into your breakfast choices on a regular basis.

Summary

THEME III
Feel Your Body
Energize Your Body and Increase Vitality

Strategy #10: Slow Down
Strategy #11: Move Your Body
Strategy #12: Fuel Your Body

Self-care is such an integral part of your well-being and happiness. *You need to take care of yourself before you can be at your best to take care of others.*

Taking the time to connect with your body is important. Your body needs

- nutrients as fuel for energy;
- movement to keep agile and fluid;
- down time to release stress;
- sleep to rebuild tissues and organs; and
- hydration to keep things flowing.

Neglecting any of these aspects can have impacts on your health, how you feel, and your overall vitality.

Nurture Your Relationships

STRATEGY #13

Deepen Your Connections

The most basic and powerful way to connect to
another person is to listen. Just listen. Perhaps the
most important thing we ever give each other is our
attention.... A loving silence often has far more power
to heal and to connect than the most well-intentioned
words.

—Rachel Naomi Remen

A deep need for a human is a sense of connection, of
belonging, of feeling loved.
*One of the biggest and most important relationships
you'll ever have is with yourself.* It supersedes all other relationships.
It's important that you take the time to nourish this relationship.

Your spirituality is a significant part of that relationship, that
is, being connected with something bigger than you—your source,
your creator. This often gets confused with religion. Being spiritual
does not require you to believe or follow a religion but can be
cultivated through religion. Whether you refer to your source as
the universe, the cosmos, spirit, or God doesn't matter. Having a
spiritual connection can bring you peace. *Developing your spiritual*

connection may be the most profound relationship you'll ever experience in this lifetime.

Relationships with others are also important for connection. Sometimes even when someone is among others, they still feel disconnected and alone. They may be close to people in the physical sense, but there is no emotional connection.

Some people have supportive, loving, and deeply connected families. Others do not. They're simply floating around in the world, feeling completely alone.

Think of the movie *Castaway,* starring Tom Hanks as Chuck Noland. Hanks is stranded on a desert island after a plane crash. He has no one to connect with, so he takes a volleyball that he finds, draws a face on it and calls it Wilson. Wilson becomes his companion. Feeling that connection is an important part of what gives him the drive to live on for such a long time.

Community is another way to get a sense of belonging. Communities come in many forms, such as organized religion, sports teams, or groups of people with similar interests or hobbies. Joining a community is a great way to feel connection. Choose a community that aligns with your values and personal interests.

I recently attended a house concert that was a fundraiser for a young person who was undergoing a transgender operation. I was excited because it was my first house concert, and happy that the donation was supporting someone to find their place in this world. I was completely blown away by the support this individual received from his family. Most transgender individuals are rejected by their families and lead very difficult and lonely lives. The father and one of the brothers were part of the band. Another brother sang a song with the band. His sister, who doesn't sing, dedicated and sang a song in front of the entire gathering. It was very heartwarming to be a spectator to the deep human connection I was witnessing.

In relationships communication plays a vital part of building and sustaining the connection. Often people are so caught up in their own stuff. Even when they're with people, they don't stop and listen to the other person. They're busy thinking about what they have to do afterward or what their next response will be. They don't take the time to listen to the person they're with. How are they? What are they up to? What challenges or exciting things are happening for them?

A healthy relationship has good communication. Both parties contribute to the conversation and are open to listening to the other. They respect the other person's perspective. They don't need to agree with it, just honor it. They're truly engaged and interested in the other person.

If you're feeling lonely, take a look around you. Which relationship is the most important one to you? Start strengthening that relationship today.

By nurturing all of your relationships, with self and others, you will feel more connected to life.

Exercise

To develop expand your connection with someone and make them feel you're there for them, do this.

1. The next time you're with someone, stop thinking about your stuff.
2. Put down your cell phone.
3. Don't reply to e-mails or text messages.
4. Be present and listen to them.
5. Listen and engage in the conversation.
6. Be curious about them.
7. Ask them personal questions that show you're listening.

8. Paraphrase their words and get confirmation that you understand what they're saying.

Doing this provides a valuable gift to that person, and they will feel that sense of connection.

The Power of Touch

Too often we underestimate the power of a touch,
a smile, a kind word, a listening ear, an honest
compliment, or the smallest act of caring, all of which
have the potential to turn a life around.

—Leo F. Buscaglia

*A*n important aspect we get out of our relationships is touch.
They say that babies who aren't touched will die. They
simply cannot survive without physical touch.

Some families are all about physical touch. They hug one
another on a regular basis. They express their love and support
for one another through physical touch. They hold one another in
times of sorrow. Other families don't express themselves through
physical touch as much.

My family was one of those where there was not much
physical touch. When I was younger and we went to church, I was
uncomfortable shaking the other people's hands when the priest
asked us to turn around and shake hands with our neighbors and
say, "Peace be with you." To this day reaching out and touching
others is something that I need to consciously think of. It's not that

I don't care about people—I care very deeply. It simply means that it doesn't come naturally to me.

I was once taught a heart hug. When you hug a person, his or her head is to the left of yours. Most humans have their physical heart on the left side of the chest. Hugging this way is a connection between your physical hearts that raises the energy of the hug to a whole new level.

There is nothing like the power of human touch when it's genuine and coming from a place of caring. You can't beat it!

Exercise

If you're craving more physical touch in your life, do this.

1. In the next week, when you feel the urge to hug someone, do it. Make it a heart hug.
2. Do it from a placing of genuine caring. Really hold the other person, instead of giving a weak hug where you're barely touching each other.
3. Some people may feel uncomfortable receiving hugs; honor and respect that. Asking someone first if they're open to accepting a hug can help ease their discomfort and is respectful.

The more you give hugs, the more comfortable you'll become with physical touch. You will feel a stronger sense of connection with others.

STRATEGY #15

Surround Yourself with Great People

Surround yourself with positive people that are doing positive things in life, and see how it will change your life for the better.

—Anonymous

The five people we surround ourselves with the most, whether we are conscious of it or not, influence us. We model their traits, behaviors and aspirations.

Who do you have in your life? Are you where you want to be? Are you who you want to be?

One of the best ways to get to where you want to be in life is to learn from someone who's already there. You don't need to figure out the path on your own. They have already done it for you. They have gone through all the challenges and are where you want to be. You can ask them how they got there and teach you what they have done. This is what having a mentor is.

Other people you may want to surround yourself with are people who display traits that you admire and aspire to be. The more you're around them, the more you'll display those traits.

Exercise

Reach out to someone new who could mentor you or who inspires you.

1. This week identify someone whom you admire and want to be more like, someone you want to learn from.
2. Reach out to them and make a connection. It may seem risky, but it's worth it. You'll never know the outcome if you don't try.

By taking the action yourself, you'll surround yourself with people that inspire you, teach you, and give you enjoyment.

Summary

THEME IV
Nurture Your Relationships
Develop Heartfelt Connections

Strategy #13: Deepen Your Connections
Strategy #14: The Power of Touch
Strategy #15: Surround Yourself with Great People

Relationships, physical touch, and connection are important aspects to our lives. Too many of us live a lonely life, and it doesn't need to be that way.

It does take courage to step out of your comfort zone and reach out. Some people will be receptive, and others will not.

Relationships can take many forms: with yourself, significant others, partners, spouses, children, family, friends, co-workers, acquaintances, mentors, or even, at times, strangers that are only passing through our lives for a brief moment.

Surrounding yourself with people who inspire you and whom you admire will propel you in becoming the person you want to be.

Uncover Your Happiness

How to Begin

> To accomplish great things, we must not only act, but also dream; not only plan, but also believe.
> —Anatole France

If you have read through the entire book and feel like you have a lot of areas where you can improve, don't be hard on yourself. *We all have room for improvement and growth; nobody's perfect.*

You're amazing and lovable just how you are right now! It doesn't matter where you have come from or what you have done; that is the past. You can take action now to make changes for the future. *Believe it's possible! Believe in yourself!*

Nobody can want or make the changes for you. It's up to you to uncover your happiness and only you. You have to want it, and you have to do the work. *It's a choice, your choice!*

The following four sections will guide you step-by-step on how to begin.

1. Start Where You Are
    - Determine your most important strategies and the strategy to adopt at this time.
2. Focus on What You Want
    - Get more clarity surrounding the strategy you have chosen to adopt.
3. Take Inspired Action
    - Create your action plan to successfully adopt the strategy.
4. Find Support
    - Keep yourself on track with a support system.

Start Where You Are

> Start where you are. Use what you have. Do what you can.
> —Arthur Ashe

We all have to start where we are. There's no other way.

Don't focus all at once on all of the strategies you want to adopt. It will be overwhelming. When I get overwhelmed I shut down and become stuck. I don't want that to happen to you. Pick one strategy to adopt. Once you're satisfied with that one strategy, adopt another.

Life is always changing, and so are you. Because you already worked on a strategy some time ago doesn't mean that you'll never explore it again. It's perfectly fine to keep on working on what is most important to you at the time, even if that means diving back into a strategy you worked on before.

Exercise

The following exercise will assist you in determining which strategies are most important to you and the one to adopt at this time.

1. Ask yourself, "What does success feel like in each of the fifteen strategies?" The themes and strategies are listed below for your reference.
   - Describe it in terms of what you feel, hear, and see.
   - What will you be doing once you achieve success?
   - What will your life be like?
   - What will your relationships be like?
2. Rank your level of satisfaction for each of the strategies on a level from 1 to 10, with 1 being completely unsatisfied and 10 being completely satisfied.
   - Take some time to reflect; don't simply assign a 5 to everything.

3. Look at your rankings.
   - Are there any surprises for you?
4. Now that you know what success feels like and you have ranked your level of satisfaction for each strategy, put a star beside strategies that are most important to you.
5. Out of your important strategies, pick one to adopt.
   - A good place to start is with the strategy that has the lowest level of satisfaction.

Your next step is to gain more clarity about the strategy you're adopting.

Themes and Strategies

Master Yourself
1. Start with Gratitude
2. Change Your Perception of the World
3. Get Rid of the Negative Self-Talk
4. Acknowledge Yourself
5. Forgiveness Is Key

Live with Integrity
6. Discover Your Emotions
7. Take Responsibility for Yourself
8. Live by Your Values
9. Find Your Purpose

Feel Your Body
10. Slow Down
11. Move Your Body
12. Fuel Your Body

Nurture Your Relationships
13. Deepen Your Connections
14. The Power of Touch
15. Surround Yourself with Great People

Focus on What You Want

Some pursue happiness, others create it.

—Anonymous

It's important to *focus on what you want, not what you don't want.* Often when you ask people what they want, they give you a list of what they don't want. This is common in today's society.

Focusing on what you want will give you more clarity surrounding the strategy you are adopting. It will strengthen you vision of success for that strategy.

Exercise

Get more clarity about the strategy you are adopting by contrasting it against what you don't want.

1. Get a sheet of paper.
2. At the top of the page, write the name of the strategy.
3. Draw a vertical line down the middle, creating two columns.
4. In the top of the left-hand column, write "Not Wanted."
5. In the top of the right-hand column, write "Wanted."
6. In the "Not Wanted" column, list all the things that you no longer want for the strategy, one after the other.
   - Use the other side of the paper if you need it.
   - For example, "I don't want to doubt myself."
7. Once you have completed listing all the things you don't want, start back at the top of your list.
8. Look at your first item in the "Not Wanted" list, and ask yourself "What is the opposite of that?" Write that down in the "Wanted" column across from that item.
   - Be as specific as possible.

For example, write, "I have confidence in myself," where confidence is the opposite of doubt.

- You should believe that each item is achievable. If not, reword it to make it believable. For example, instead of saying "I have . . ." you could phrase it in the terms as "I'm in the process of . . ."

9. Cross out the "Not Wanted" item.

10. Move to the next item on the "Not Wanted" list. Determine the opposite, write it down, and cross out the "Not Wanted" item.

11. Keep doing this until you have worked through all of your "Not Wanted" items.

12. Fold your paper in half and just look at the "Wanted" side.

- This is what you want. This is your vision of success for yourself and for this strategy.

Your next step is to determine which actions to take, your action plan.

Tip: This 'Wanted/Not Wanted' process can be adapted and used for anything you want more clarity on.

Take Inspired Action

> Change begins with the first step.
> —Suzanne Rivard

Now that you know which strategy you are adopting and have clarity, you need to take action. Simply wishing it's not enough. *It's up to you to uncover your happiness, to create the life you want and deserve.*

If the strategy you identified to adopt seems too daunting, break it down into more manageable chunks. *Create your action plan.*

Exercise

To determine your list of actions, answer the following questions.

1. Looking at your vision of success and what you want, what is your overall goal?
2. What do you want to achieve overall for that goal?
3. What actions could you take to move yourself forward?
   - Include the strategy exercise provided as an action step if you haven't completed it yet.
4. What would be the smallest or easiest first step for you?
5. Who else could assist you in completing your actions?
6. What are three actions you could take that would make sense for you this week?

Once you have completed your list of actions, answer the following questions.

7. When will you do those actions? Write the specific day beside the action.
8. On a scale of 1 to 10, how likely are you to complete each action, with 1 being not committed and 10 being totally committed?

- If the answer is below an 8, then ask what is stopping you from completing the action. Make this your first action.

9. If you normally sabotage yourself, what will you do differently this time?
10. Whom will you tell about your actions (to support you in completing them)?
11. How will you know you've completed your actions?
12. How will you reward yourself when you complete your actions?

You now have an action plan to successfully adopt the strategy.

Your next step is to ensure that you have a support system in place.

Find Support

> You can't see the frame when you are in the picture.
> —Brian Tracy

You don't need to do this all alone. In fact, you don't want to.

There may be some things that you want to keep private, and that's okay. There are other things where it's vital to be around people that support you and your efforts to make improvements in your life. They offer you a perspective that you cannot see yourself. If people don't support you, if they put you down or tell you that it's a waste of time, it will be much harder for you to make changes. You can have many supports. *Find at least one person that can support you.*

Connect with a friend, a family member, or someone that you can talk with in a safe way, where you're not judged for what you're experiencing and are allowed to express exactly what you're feeling. He or she can be your sounding board, offer you another perspective, and comfort you when things are challenging. If you get off your path, this person can remind you of what you want. You might also seek out other options if necessary: maybe a religious or spiritual group, a coach, a counselor, or a therapist. There are so many groups and programs out there. Look for them.

Someone that you can vent to is also supportive. I have never vented all that much, because I didn't believe it was right. I thought it meant that I was complaining and judgmental. Venting is actually a very healthy thing to do. Complaining is what keeps you stuck.

Venting honors your feelings. It allows you to clear your head, release expectations, and come up with a solution. It's about expressing to someone what you're feeling—the good, the bad, and the ugly. You don't want the other person to help you or offer you advice. You just need to get what you think and feel off your chest, and then you can let it go. Complaining is something quite different. It's about expressing resentment or displeasure, and perhaps seeking sympathy. It's not about releasing tension or finding solutions. It's just grumbling.

If you're going to vent to someone, then you want to have a conversation with them beforehand. You want someone who is supportive, someone you trust. Ask them if they will be your venting partner, which means that you'll ask their permission to vent to them and that all they do is listen. They don't need to fix you or your problem or come up with possible solutions. They just need to be there for you. Agree to a time limit, and stick to it so that you don't ramble on, five minutes is often enough. I wouldn't go past fifteen minutes. If you're finding that you're venting often, you want to seek out more than one venting partner or a professional to support you. Too much venting with one person can be very taxing for that person.

Summary

Uncover Your Happiness
Be the Creative Force of Your Life

How to Begin
Start Where You Are
Focus on What You Want
Take Inspired Action
Find Support

With your strategy identified, a clear vision of success and what you want, your action steps, and support in place, you are now prepared to successfully adopt your strategy. *It's time to take action! It's time to uncover your happiness!*

Once you are satisfied with this strategy, come back to *Start Where You Are* to determine your next strategy.

Final Note from Suzanne

What I have shared in this book are strategies in my life that have made a difference. Focusing on improvements in any one of these strategies has impacted my life for the better and brought me more happiness.

I feel that self-development, discovery, and awareness are part of a lifelong journey. I always have things that I want to improve on and growth areas. Nobody is perfect. That's what keeps life interesting. It's the ups and downs that keep us growing into better people. A world full of perfect people would be boring.

I live a much happier life than in the past. It has taken me years of challenging life experiences to discover all of these strategies. I hope that sharing them with you in one place will assist you in identifying the areas in your life that you want to make improvements in, and that the exercises provided expedite achieving your goals and dreams.

I leave you with one last thought, a quote from Yoda.

"No! Try not. Do, or do not. There is no try."

Happiness is a choice, not a destination. May your life be one of much happiness!

Suzanne

CPSIA information can be obtained at www.ICGtesting.com
Printed in the USA
LVOW07s0119030214

371855LV00001B/3/P